To Thomas and Lenore

THE VIEW FROM POINT LOOKOUT

The story of Bill Spargo's Queensland retirement

First published by Busybird Publishing 2026

ISBN:

Paperback: 978-1-923501-81-2

Front cover image: Whale Rock, Point Lookout - Stephen Whiteside

Back cover image: Sunrise over Point Lookout - Stephen Whiteside

Cover design: Fiona Sinclair

Layout and typesetting: Busybird Publishing

Busybird Publishing
2/118 Para Road
Montmorency, Victoria
Australia 3094
www.busybird.com.au

Contents

Introduction

In 2024 I published a book, 'Snow, Fire and Gold - the story of Bill Spargo and Evelyn Piper's life in the Australian mountains.' The book was inspired by a visit I had made to 'Spargo's Hut', a remote, one-room hut above the snowline, near Mt Hotham, in 1982. Although abandoned for many years, the hut had remained crammed full of all the items necessary for everyday living, and I had resolved to discover the story of the people who have lived in it - William Benjamin ('Bill') Spargo and his English born wife, Evelyn Maud Piper.

Spargo's Hut in 1982
The structure over the front door is likely a remnant of two extra rooms constructed by Harold Maddison.

I learnt that Bill had been born in Bairnsdale in 1888 and had spent his childhood there. However, the family moved to the inner Melbourne suburb of Brunswick while he was still young. He had left home in his teens, and moved to northeast Victoria where his grandfather, Benjamin, had been very active in the pursuit of gold in the 19th century. Bill had mostly been employed as a road worker, but his passion had been the pursuit of gold. In 1921 he had been appointed head of the road gang working between Omeo and Mt Hotham, and had been responsible for founding the Hotham ski resort in 1925. He had built the hut now known as Spargo's Hut in 1933, as a base for gold prospecting. He had survived the 1939 bushfire in the hut, and discovered a rich gold reef, which he called the Red Robin, on Machinery Spur near Mt Hotham, the following year. He had also discovered another gold reef, which he called the One Alone, though this was nowhere near as productive.

Bill Spargo

Evelyn had shared many of these experiences with Bill (though not the bushfire), and they had married in 1946. Alas, the marriage had not been a success, however. They sold the Red Robin Mine in 1952, split the proceeds equally, and went their separate ways - Evelyn back to her family in England, Bill to Point Lookout on North Stradbroke Island in Queensland. 'Snow, Fire and Gold' ends here. This book tells the story of what happened next - at least as far as Bill is concerned.

Evelyn Piper

So where does the information come from?

Bill Spargo sold his hut (or 'cabin', as he called it) to Harold Maddison, who operated the Buffalo View Hotel in the small town of Porepunkah, near Bright, in the Ovens Valley. Maddison was also interested in the pursuit of gold and, like Bill, planned to use the hut as a base for prospecting. (Unfortunately, I do not have a photo of him.)

I began the research for 'Snow, Fire and Gold' in 1987. I was concerned at the time that the Mt Hotham Alpine Resort might build a ski tow up to somewhere near Spargo's Hut. I felt this would spell the end of the hut and decided to do what I could to protect it. I rang the resort, explaining that I was interested in the hut. I think the resort was probably hoping at the time that the hut would fall down, and that the person I spoke to tried to discourage me.

"Do you realise it's privately owned?" he asked me.

"No," I replied. "I didn't know that. Can you tell me who the owner is then?"

After a brief hesitation, I was given the name of Nancye Sullivan, who lived in Bright, and her phone number. I rang Nancye and told her I had been told she owned Spargo's Hut.

Her reply astonished me.

"You are kidding me?" she said. "I have been trying to prove this all my life, and nobody believes me!"

Nancye went on to explain that she was the daughter of Harold Maddison. He had died in 1972. Her father had tried to establish the hut as a holiday home for the family, but it had not been a success. She recalled one time when, as a child, she had been left alone in the hut to wash the dishes. There had been a howling wind outside, and she had been absolutely terrified. She did not have good memories of the hut.

Nevertheless, as an adult, she had attempted to reassert the family's claim on it. She told me that her father had been paying rates annually - first to the Shire of Omeo, then to the Shire of Bright. Payments had ceased following his death. There had been fires in both offices, and the records of payment had been lost. Nancye had been sending annual rate payments to the Shire of Bright, but they were being returned. She had been told the period of non-payment had been too long. I told Nancye I would give her as much support as I could, though there was not much I could do. I successfully nominated Spargo's Hut for registration with the Historic Buildings Council (now Heritage Victoria). The resort management supported the application, though did drag its heels somewhat initially. I also do not have a photograph of Nancye.

Following the sale of the hut to Maddison and Bill's move to Stradbroke Island, the two men had corresponded regularly. Nancye very generously gave me the letters that her father had received from Bill. These proved to be a real treasure trove, and a great starting point for this book. (Sadly, Harold's letters to Bill would appear to have been lost. At least one of Bill's letters to Harold is also missing.) She also gave me other valuable documents relating to Bill, her father and the hut. You will see I have quoted directly from Bill's letters to Harold from time to time. (These are in italics.) Bill's grammar leaves something to be desired, but I have left it in its original form for the sake of authenticity.

One of the men I interviewed for what became 'Snow, Fire and Gold' was Ted Staff. Ted, an SEC linesman by profession, had worked for Bill as a cook at the Red Robin Mine during the summer of 1949/50, while on long service leave. He had also visited Bill at Stradbroke Island, and was able to tell me much about Bill's life there. Ted's older brother Norm had also worked at the mine and had also visited Bill in Queensland. (Norm, with his wife, Lillian, had purchased the Red Robin from Bill and Evelyn in 1952. He had died prior to the commencement of my research, however.)

In 1988, I spoke on the telephone to two long-term residents of Point Lookout, Ellie Durbidge and Dr Robert Paterson. Both had known Bill and were able to give me information about his time there. Several other people had snippets of information, some of which I have been able to weave into this book.

Finally, I visited Point Lookout for a week in September 2025. This proved invaluable and gave me a sense of how the island might have changed since Bill's day, as well as some understanding of the ways in which it probably had not changed very much at all. While there, I met long term North Stradbroke resident Gwennie Specht. Gwennie introduced me to a book written by a close friend of hers, Beryl Moore. Titled 'Island Eden - Point Lookout and its Pioneers', it contains a small chapter about 'Mr Spargo'. (Beryl has since passed away.) Gwennie has a dim and distant memory of meeting 'Mr Spargo' herself when she was a teenager.

Most of the stories are based on events I have either been told or read about. I have fictionalised these slightly, but only to flesh them out a little and make them more engaging to the reader. I have occasionally created conversations that I believe are likely to be similar to other conversations that probably did take place. Occasionally I have imagined the stories myself, based on what I have learnt about Bill and his most unusual life. For example, I have no evidence that Bill ever climbed Mt Bippo, but the walk is so popular amongst island residents that it seems highly likely that he would have.

Despite my initial fears that the Mt Hotham Alpine Resort had no interest in Spargo's Hut, it has been very heartening in recent years to see that it now values the hut and is keen to protect it. The Resort arranged for the hut to be wrapped in protective aluminium foil during the highly destructive bushfires of 2019/20. Then, during the refurbishment of Spargo's Hut by the Victorian High Country Huts Association in 2021, the Resort funded a helicopter to transfer important building supplies to the site. Numerous smaller items have also been taken from the hut by the Resort to prevent pilfering. These are now held under lock and key at Hotham. It is to be hoped that they will eventually be made available for public display. Indeed, attitudes to Spargo's Hut over time have mirrored community attitudes to the high country huts more generally. Where once they were seen as ugly blots on the natural landscape, they are now highly valued as symbolic reminders of the rich cultural heritage they represent.

Here, then, is 'The View from Point Lookout - the story of Bill Spargo's Queensland retirement.' It has been a great joy to write, and I hope the reading of it brings some pleasure also.

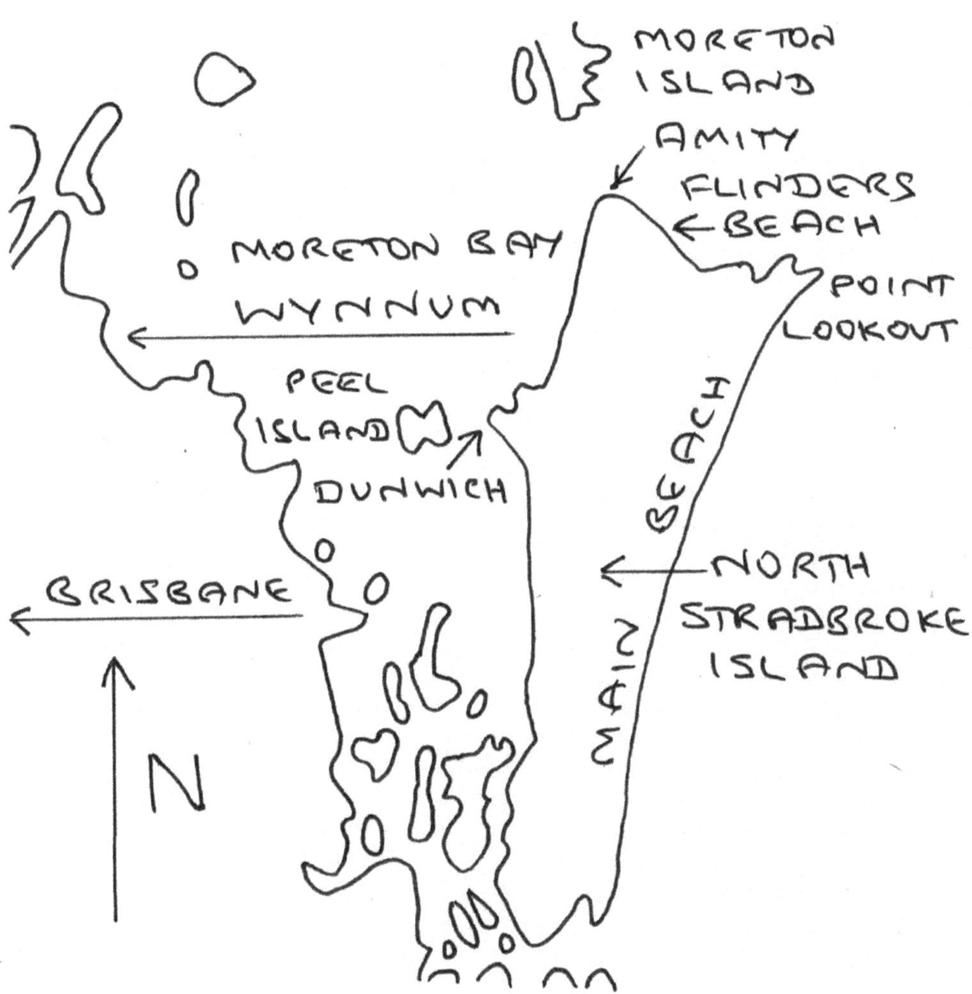

Map of North Stradbroke Island

1
Elsie

Elsie looked across the table to her older brother. He was haughty - something of a snob, really. He wasn't a bad man, though. Indeed, he had many admirable qualities. Besides, he was her older brother. That was reason enough to love him.

Sunlight streamed through the window. It was warm, but that was nothing unusual. This was Brisbane, after all. No doubt many saw Bill as the black sheep of the family. He had abandoned city and family life to live as a recluse in the bush. Yet in some ways, surely, Elsie herself was the black sheep. She was the only one of the four siblings to have left Victoria and make a life for herself in another state. Polly and Cecil lived in Melbourne. She had raised a family here. She had no regrets. Brisbane had been good to her.

Bill had been visiting her for a few weeks in the winter months for several years now - ever since he had discovered that rich gold reef and had had the means to escape from the depths of the Victorian high country winters. Yet she knew the city life did not suit him - cars, traffic, noise, pollution and crowds of people. These were the very things he had sought escape from at Mt Hotham. He enjoyed Brisbane's warmth, but in every other respect, it was not really the place for him.

Inspiration struck her.

"Bill, I've been thinking."

He looked up, quizzically.

"You love the Queensland heat, but not the city, right?"

He nodded.

“Well, why not try to find some patch of the Queensland bush to live in? Combine the Queensland climate with those qualities you love so much at Mt Hotham - the isolation, the closeness to nature, the general peace and quiet.”

Bill was all ears now.

“Sounds great, Elsie, but where? Do you have a place in mind?”

“Perhaps,” she replied thoughtfully. “I’ve heard good things about Stradbroke Island - Point Lookout, in particular. It’s pretty rough, but there is a small settlement there. You’d be close to the ocean, with plenty of lonely beaches to explore, and a whole new array of fauna and flora for you to investigate. It’s not too far from Brisbane, either. You could still visit me from time to time. It might be just the thing,”

Bill said nothing, but his eyes sparkled in a way she had not seen for a long time.

Bill Spargo at the Red Robin Mine, around 1950

2
The Wangaratta Ski Club

Bill Callander immediately recognised the trim, neatly groomed figure of Bill Spargo as he approached the counter of his family's large general store in Murphy Street, Wangaratta.

"What can I do for you, Bill?

As President of the Wangaratta Ski Club, Callander knew that not everybody who entered the store was there to make a purchase. Often, they were there to discuss ski business. Such was the case today.

"I'm leaving the area, Bill, and I'd like somebody to buy my cabin and keep it going. I have a permissive occupancy there. The area around my cabin offers potentially the best ski jumping in Australia. You know you can ski downhill pretty much anywhere, but really good sites for jumping are very rare."

He quoted a figure - a low figure, but a figure nonetheless. He was not offering to give his cabin away.

Callander nodded thoughtfully.

"Fair enough, Bill. I'll take it to the committee and let you know what they say."

Privately, though, he was not confident. It was hard enough getting to Mt St Bernard, where the Wangaratta Ski Club had built its lodge. The prospect of travelling on to Mt Hotham - and beyond - to reach Bill Spargo's cabin was not enticing.

Sure enough, in due course, the Wangaratta Ski Club committee agreed they could see no great use for Bill Spargo's cabin, and Bill Callander informed him of their decision.

3
Harold

Harold Maddison lay in bed beside his wife, Lilias, at the end of another long, hard day. Their work as operators of the Buffalo View Hotel at Porepunkah was not necessarily frantic - although on occasions it was exactly that - but it was constant, and unremitting. Harold was becoming increasingly aware of the need for an outlet of some sort.

"I've heard that Bill Spargo is keen to sell his cabin, Lil."

"Are you thinking of buying it?"

"Yes, I am."

Lilias paused before answering. "Why?"

"Well, it would be exciting to find some gold. I'm told Bill found quite a lot of gold there before he discovered the Red Robin. It's pretty rough now, I know, but it has great potential. We could put a road in, lighting, hot water, the lot. It would be a great project for the whole family. I reckon the boys would love a challenge like that."

Lilias wasn't so sure. She'd heard it was very remote, and the weather was extremely unpredictable. It could be very wild. On the other hand, she knew Harold was struggling with the day-to-day demands of the hotel. Most of the work had already fallen onto her. He certainly needed some more enjoyable activity to distract him from the hotel, but surely this was a bit extreme.

"I don't know, Harold. I'm not convinced. I guess it's up to you."

Harold lay on his back in bed in silence for some time.

"Good night, Lil."

"Good night, Harold."

Buffalo View Hotel, Porepunkah
Built in 1870, it was demolished in 1971.
Courtesy of the National Trust of Australia (Victoria)

4
A Different Kind of Prospecting

Bill surveyed the land around him with a critical eye. He knew well enough there was no gold to be found on Stradbroke Island. This island was mostly sand, with a few rocky outcrops here and there. People didn't expect much of it - other than the sand, of course, which was of considerable value in itself. The island had been around for a while, though. That got Bill thinking. Long enough for countless generations of plants to live and die. He paced around Fern Gully Lagoon. All this water, all this vegetation. Surely...

He walked on, eyes fixed on the ground. Nothing but sand and low-lying vegetation. Soon he came to an eroded gully...bingo! There it was! A dark patch where the overlying sand had been washed away by water. He walked across to it and bent down to examine it closely. Sure enough, it looked very much like peat!

He returned the next day with a shovel. It was time for some serious excavation. This was remote country. He hadn't seen anybody anywhere near the lagoon yesterday, and didn't expect to today, either. He began once again with the walk along Flinders Beach from Point Lookout. He loved this long stretch of sand and was already coming to know it well. There was a very rough track running through the bush, but Bill preferred to walk along the water's edge. Still some way short of Amity Point, however, he turned inland to the lagoon. It was rough country, all right, with a towering sand dune off to one side.

It didn't take him long to find the spot he had found yesterday. He started digging straight away. After turning over a few shovelfuls, he paused to look more closely at the material he was digging up. This was peat all right! It was very moist, and poor quality, but no doubt it would be drier, and better, at depth. Moreover, he was likely to find it at many other sites around the lagoon. He felt sure of that.

Bill quivered with excitement as he began the long walk back along the beach to home, shovel resting on his shoulder. That familiar thrill of discovery coursed through his veins once again. It wasn't gold - far from it - but it was still something. Would he be a hero again? Probably not. Still, it had the potential to significantly improve the quality of life of the residents of the island and improve his standing among them. That was a good feeling.

5
Sea Spinach and Watercress

Bill was on the hunt for fresh greens. His diet of dried fruit - apricots, raisins and sultanas - served him well, and was healthy, but it was also quite monotonous. Besides, everybody needs fresh greens. First, he walked out to the headland beside North Gorge. He knew there was a plentiful supply of sea spinach growing out there. Also known as warrigal greens, he had heard that Sir Joseph Banks had served this same plant on the Endeavour to ward off scurvy amongst the crew. Captain Cook cast a long shadow. He had even given Point Lookout its name! Bill harvested a good supply and filled a sack he was carrying with him. He would not eat any now, though. He knew it had to be steamed before it was safe for eating. Next, he picked his way slowly down to the head of the gorge where a freshwater spring supported a large crop of watercress. He filled a second sack with this. He then headed home, carrying what was by now quite a significant burden. An unusual looking plant caught his eye on the return journey, and he threw some of that into one of the sacks, too.

Sunrise near North Gorge, Point Lookout

Once home, he threw down his fresh harvest onto the grass and pulled up a seat to more closely inspect this new, intriguing type of vegetation. It did not resemble anything he had seen before. Nor could he recall having heard anybody describe anything similar to this. He probably should find out more about it before eating it. He was curious, however. He'd taken risks like this before and never come to any great harm. Throwing caution to the wind, he placed some leaves in his mouth and started chewing.

*

Bill awoke to find himself lying on the ground. The stars were shining brightly, and the moon was high in the sky.

6
Pearl

"There's a vast resource of untapped peat up there, Pearl. I know there is. But I can't mine it myself. It's far too big a job for one man, or even two. My neighbour, Taylor, is as excited as I am, but we need help, and lots of it. The Queensland government are just ignoring me, Pearl. I can't believe it. They are expressing no interest whatsoever!"

Bill was back in Melbourne for a brief visit. It was good to see his old friend from Mt Hotham, Pearl Bradshaw, again.

Pearl listened sympathetically. There wasn't much she could do, but she was more than happy to lend an ear and offer encouragement. She could also give him a hot cup of tea and a piece of cake!

7
A Call from the Queensland Mines Department

The telephone rang in the office of the Victorian Mines Department. It was answered by a senior geologist. The voice on the other end sounded a long way away. The connection was not particularly good. The speaker introduced himself as a senior geologist of the Queensland Mines Department.

They explained pleasantries, then got down to business.

"Listen, we've got a fellow up here who claims to have discovered coal on Stradbroke Island. Name of Bill Spargo."

"Know him well. If Bill Spargo says there's coal on Stradbroke Island, there's coal on Stradbroke Island."

"Yeah? He seems like a rather strange sort of fellow, to be honest."

"Mate, he's a prospector. They're all a bit strange, and the better they are, the stranger they get. He discovered a rich gold reef down here, but I reckon he'd be able to sniff out anything of value."

"Oh, I see. Fair enough. OK. Thanks."

"No worries. Should go well for you."

"OK. Thanks again."

8
Letter to Harold 29th April 1954

Harold opened his letter from Bill Spargo with a mixture of excitement and relief. They had agreed to correspond regularly, but Harold had been starting to have some doubts. It had been a month since he had sent his letter. Bill was such a busy man, and something of a celebrity. Would he really be interesting in writing to the likes of him? Besides, his new life would be so full of interest, surely his memories of Mt Hotham would quickly start to fade?

Apparently not. Bill expressed genuine interest in Harold's life, and his plans for the cabin at Little Plains. He said he had found Harold's sketch of the area around the cabin easy to follow and freely offered detailed advice on how and where to best find gold. That was reassuring. He didn't hold much store in Harold's plan for hydraulic sluicing, though. The gold was only ever patchy, he said, and there were too many obstacles - big boulders and snow gums - in the way. They would need to be removed, and it was hard work. No, Bill clearly thought Harold needed to get back to basics. The key, he felt, was to wash all the surface gravel off down to the solid rock, leave it to drain and dry, then scrape the rock, paying particular attention to the deep crevasses. These scrapings should then be put through a sluice box to extract the gold. He advised washing off as much of the gravel as possible in the springtime, when water was plentiful, then commencing the slow scraping process during the drier months of summer. He made the point that most of the gold was in the top eighteen inches, so there wasn't much point in digging any deeper.

What is hydraulic sluicing?

Hydraulic sluicing is a method used to extract gold grains from clay or gravel sometimes buried beneath non-gold bearing ground. It requires a steady flow of water, and a drop in altitude to allow the water to build up a head of pressure. The water is passed through a series of progressively narrower pipes or hoses until a narrow, powerful jet shoots out of a nozzle at great speed. This jet can first be directed to tear away any barren dirt or gravel covering the gold-bearing material. Once the auriferous ground is reached, the mixture of water, mud and gravel created by the water jet can then be passed through a sluice box, which is designed to trap the dense gold grains while allowing the rest of the slurry to pass through. Hydraulic sluicing is a cheap and efficient way to mine gold, but historically has caused a tremendous amount of environmental damage.

Bill was pleased to hear that Harold was enjoying the cabin and supported his plans to put in a road. He felt this would make it a lovely place to live in during the summer months. He had instructed his solicitor to draw up an agreement, as Harold had suggested. Harold paused for reflection. He was a funny bloke, Bill - so casual. He probably wouldn't have bothered with a formal agreement at all if Harold hadn't pressed for it. Bill's solicitor had asked him for a copy of his Area Right, which he didn't currently have. He expressed concern that his papers had not arrived at Point Lookout, some four weeks after they'd been sent.

He expressed support for Harold's plans for power and lighting, with some reservations. Harold planned to install a Pelton wheel. He would run a long pipe down from near the top of Golden Point. There was a vertical drop of about one hundred feet. The water shooting out of this would spin the wheel, which would in turn drive a generator. Bill made the point that his old water race, which could provide water for the pipe leading to the Pelton wheel, had become very clogged with debris. It would take a lot of work to make it fully functional again. He suggested this would be a great summer holiday project for Harold's sons. However, Harold was not really relying on Bill's old water race. He felt a long pipe running horizontally along the contour would gather enough water from seepage.

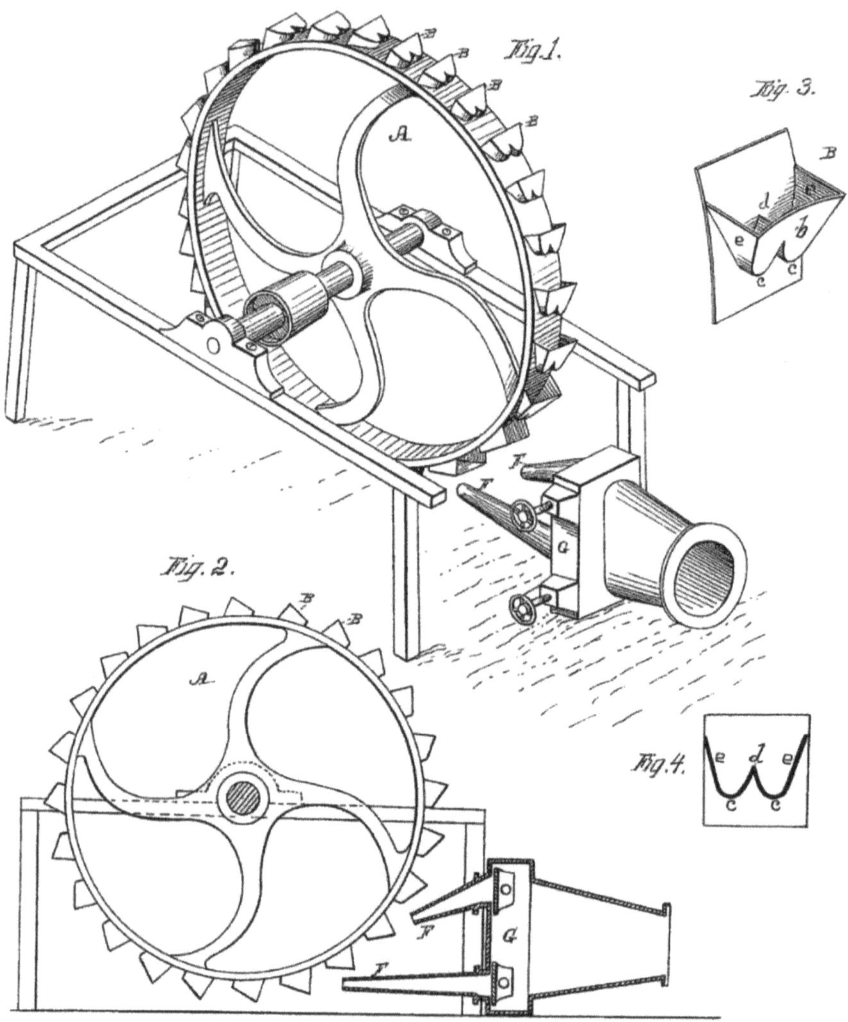

A Pelton wheel. A jet of water from the right hits the wheel and spins it. This turns the central shaft which then drives a generator. The Pelton wheel is much more efficient than earlier waterwheel designs.

These pipes, now piled behind the hut, were probably brought in by Harold for the purposes of driving the Pelton wheel.

Harold read on. Bill expressed his hope that he would be able to join Harold at the cabin the following summer to assist him. He repeated his reservations about hydraulic sluicing.

If I were you, I would try a few places by hand ground sluicing (underlined in red) *before you go to the time and expense of getting Hydraulic Sluicing plant taken out there - to be quite candid I don't think it would pay - however you try it for yourself - you can get some fine gold almost anywhere there.*

Bill also talked of his own plans. He was renovating one of the houses he was proposing to let out and installing a pump. He was also busy with his new coal field.

...in connection with the budding coal field, the Chief Govt Geologist (Q'land) will be out to look it over next month – he contacted me while I was in Melbourne and had a conference at the Vic Mines Depot about the coal with Dr. Thomas and they all seem very keen about it. We are starting a small open cut into the coal seem next week.

He ended by thanking Harold for his good wishes and offering his own in return.

Harold was encouraged by Bill's support but felt somewhat daunted by the scale of the work that appeared to lie ahead of him.

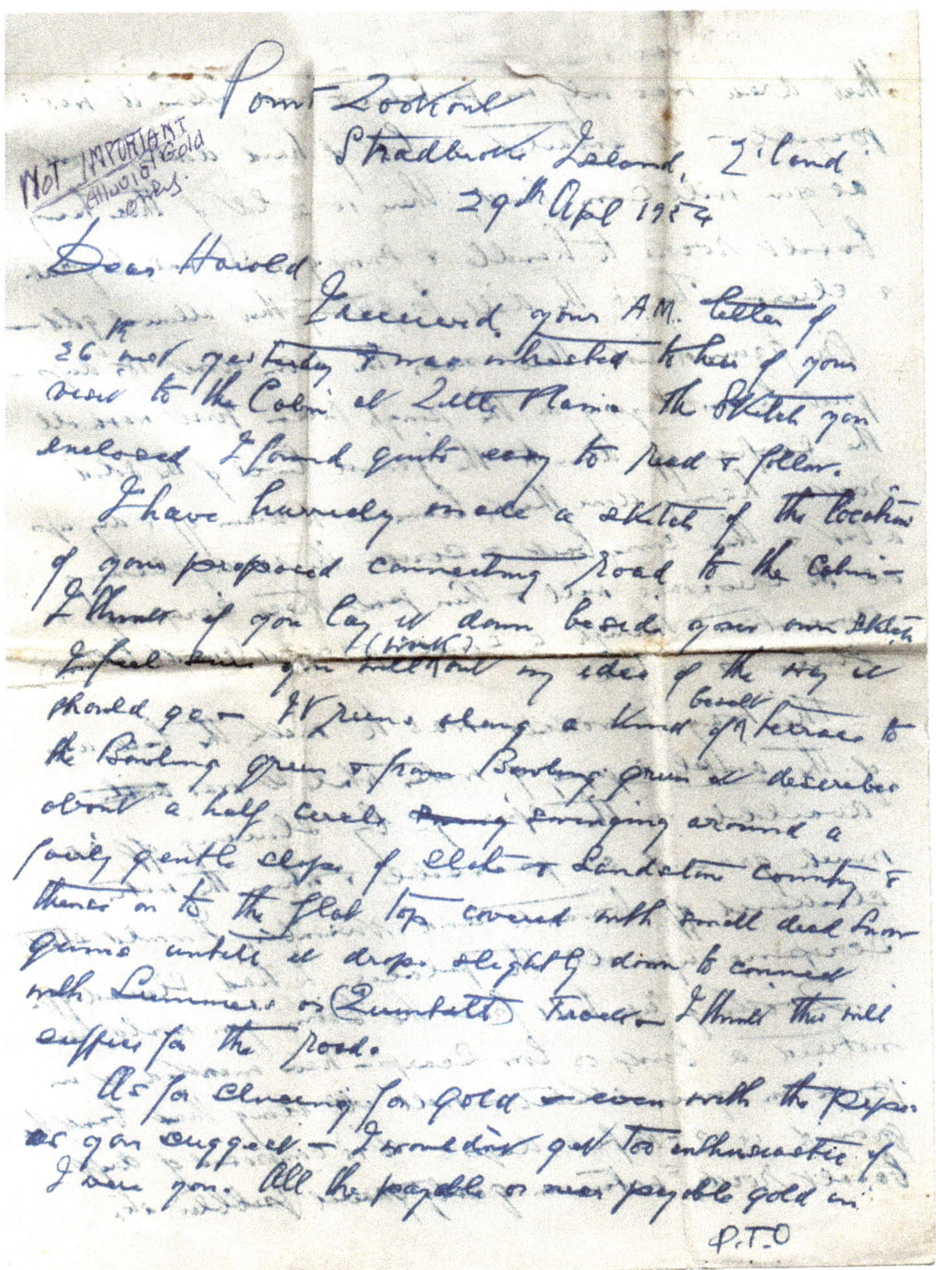

NOT IMPORTANT alluvial Gold only.

Point Lookout
Stradbroke Island, Q'land
29th April 1954

Dear Harold

I received your A.M. letter of 26th inst yesterday & was interested to hear of your visit to the Cabin at Little Plains. The sketch you enclosed I found quite easy to read & follow.

I have hurriedly made a sketch of the location of your proposed connecting Road to the Cabin. I think if you lay it down beside your own sketch I feel sure you will get my idea of the way it should go. It runs along a kind of Basalt terrace to the Bowling green & from Bowling green it describes about a half circle swinging around a fairly gentle slope of slate or sandstone country & thence on to the flat top covered with small dead brown grass until it drops slightly down to connect with Lummers or Quartett Track. I think this will suffice for the road.

As for chasing for gold — even with the Pups as you suggest — I wouldn't get too enthusiastic if I were you. All the payable or near payable gold in

P.T.O

First page of Bill's letter to Harold, 29th April 1954

The note at the top left - "NOT IMPORTANT alluvial Gold only" - is intriguing. It clearly was not written by Bill. It also does not make sense for it to have been written by Harold, because he quite definitely was interested in alluvial gold. (The handwriting is also not quite right.) I suspect it was written by some unknown third person.

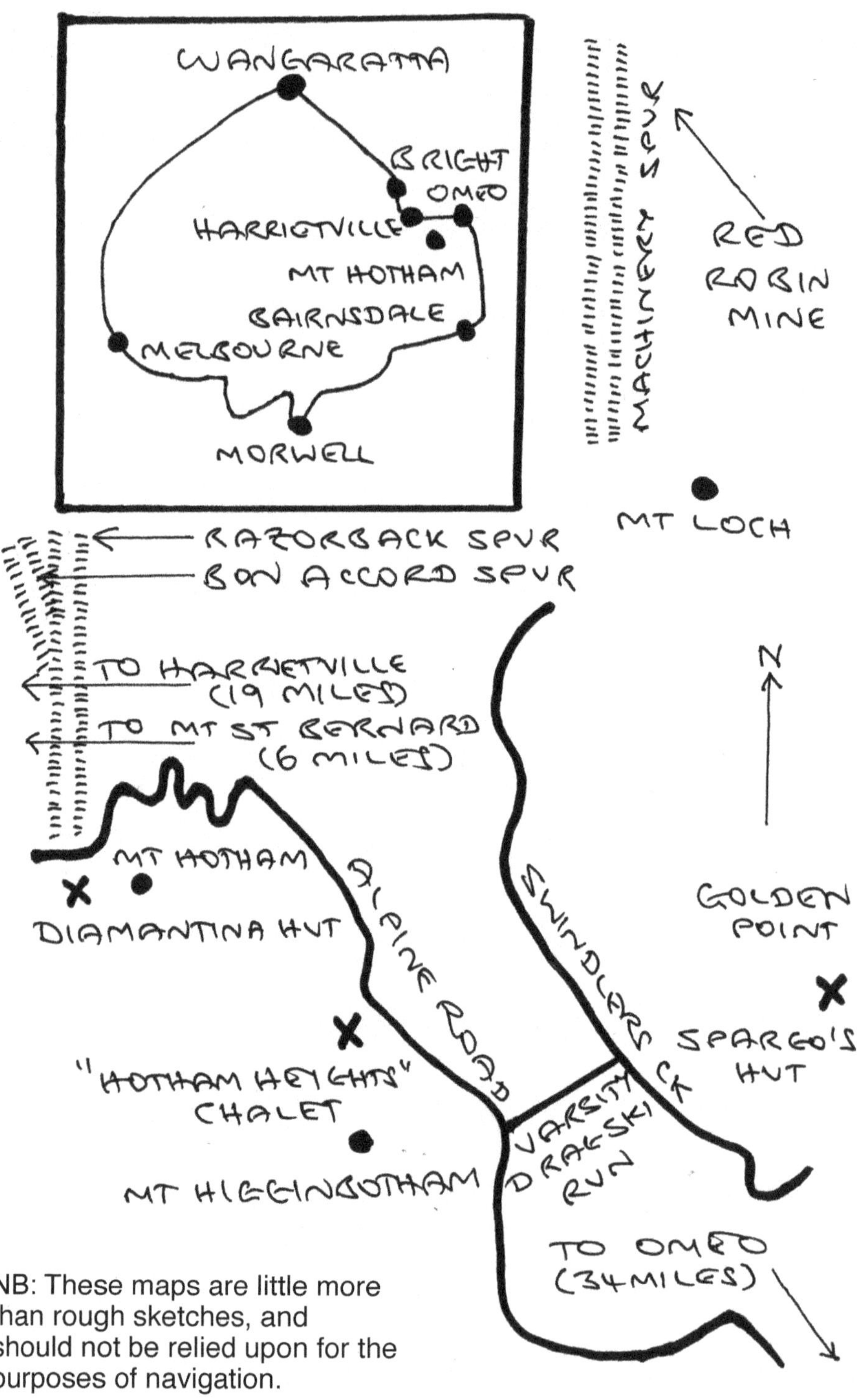

NB: These maps are little more than rough sketches, and should not be relied upon for the purposes of navigation.

9
Mt Bippo

Bill was beginning to puff now. Beads of sweat dripped off his forehead into his eyes, stinging them. He wiped them away as best he could. Bill had plenty of experience of climbing mountains, but it was the humidity he was not used to. Not long, and he'd be at the top. It was odd pacing through sand at such altitude, too. It made sense at the beach, but the idea that the whole island was little more than sand took some getting used to. The sun blazed above in a clear blue sky. Why, he thought, the air was almost as clear as a fine February day at Mt Hotham! The goanna by the side of the track down near the start of the walk had startled him for a moment. No doubt the goanna had got every much as big a scare, if not bigger!

Ah! There it was. The ocean view he had heard so much about! Yes, indeed. The locals were right. It was a breathtaking sight. The mountains in Victoria were much higher than this one, and offered many fine views, but not of the ocean. There was no particular reason for him to be here - no peat to mine, no rocks to explore, no fish to catch - but it was a fine day for a bracing walk, and everybody was telling him he must do it. Besides, it was inevitable that his natural curiosity would lead him here sooner or later. He took a bottle of water from his knapsack and took a swig. He paused a little longer to admire the view, then put the bottle back in his pack, put the pack back on his back, and turned for the return journey. He wondered whether that goanna would still be clinging to that tree, and what other surprises lay in store for him as he made his way back down.

Goanna beside the track to Mt Bippo

(The squiggly lines on the bark of the tree are the feeding trails of the larvae of the Scribbly Gum Moth.)

An elevated view of the sea from Stradbroke Island

10
A Mighty Haul

Bill stood with a friend on the beach at the water's edge, and together they cast their lines out into the surf. Almost immediately, Bill had a bite. A few moments later, so did his friend. They reeled in excitedly. What unusual fish these were, with whiskers protruding from near the mouth, and long eel-like tails. Catfish! Neither of them had ever seen them before. Tossing the two fish high onto the sand behind them, they cast again. Soon they both had another bite, another fish, and so it went all afternoon, until a great pile of dead and dying catfish lay on the beach behind them.

Eventually, the two took stock. There were far too many fish to carry home. Had their enthusiasm perhaps got the better of them? What to do next? They wandered through the bush behind the beach until they reached the sandy track that ran between Amity and Point Lookout. They could probably reach Amity in an hour. With a bit of luck, they'd be able to rouse out Bert Clayton and his truck.

*

They found Bert at the club. He was fascinated by their story, and only too happy to help. Within a couple of hours, the whole haul had been safely transferred to Point Lookout.

*

Bill served catfish at his friends' dinner table that night. He tucked in heartily but, alas, could persuade nobody else to do so. He declared them excellent eating.

Cnidoglanis macrocephalus - one of the many species of catfish that Bill might have caught

11
Letter to Harold
22nd September 1954

Harold opened the letter from Bill, which began with Bill apologising for replying so late. He remarked on how quickly the time had passed.

You spoke too of the great enthusiasm about your future plans at the cabin on the mountain - well I've been suffering from the same complaint here trying to get the two cottages knocked into shape and added to during the past month. Has been my great keenness to get the garden established as I have the best patch of land here and also have the water - am already getting some wonderful results and can now see good monetary possibilities in it...

Selling home grown vegetables? Hmm, Harold thought to himself. He must be starting to run out of money.

You know Harold your letter is like a chapter out of a book and good reading and has an almost contagious enthusiasm for future plans.

Bill talked of a small third place he was also building. It sounded unusual. He planned to place a water tank on its roof, ten feet above the ground. He spoke of the difficulty securing building materials, though. He had ordered some doors five months ago and was still waiting.

He expressed his excitement about Harold's plans for the cabin. He could picture Harold's family members, each with his own allotted task during the coming summer. He could imagine them already excited with anticipation. He again expressed his desire to be down in December to help Harold put the road in.

He expressed his surprise that the winter in Victoria had been dry, as Bill had experienced an extremely wet winter at Point Lookout. Indeed, it was the wettest he had experienced since visiting there every year since 1946. They had also experienced a cyclone every month.

...the ground is still full of water - I and my neighbour Mr Taylor began to carry out certain work on the coal seem at the beginning of the winter - we were camped out and one night a rain storm came over and there was 8 inches of rain in a few hours - we were literally washed out of the camp and our workings flooded and they have remained flooded all winter - we were hoping to get back to it again, but the rain still keeps on...

The locals were also telling Bill it had been unusually cold, but he noted that his tomatoes were still growing well and even ripening.

I have an abundance of them in the garden at present - you can grow garden stuff all the year round here so gardening is a pleasure where the soil is good.

He was expecting a drought the coming summer.

Bill told Harold that it would be a waste of time looking for uranium near Hotham.

The country rock is not the right kind. I'm not going (to) *worry about looking for it - there certainly won't be any on the island.*

He expressed surprise that Harold had heard no word from his solicitors in relation to his and Harold's agreement about the cabin and gave him their address in the city.

Will close with best wishes for a happy time on the top this coming summer.

12
A Sun-Bronzed Torso

Bill felt the power of the sun, as it beat down on his shoulders and back. It felt good. He had developed a deep tan and was not afraid of sunburn. How different was this from the chill of Mt Hotham! He had never been able to strip to the waist there. Come to think of it, there was the occasional day in summer when he could have, but his habits had been so moulded by snow, rain, sleet and wind, that it had never occurred to him to do so. There were no mountains here, either. A few hills, yes, but no mountains. Mt Bippo? They called it a mountain here, but it was really just a big hill as far as Bill was concerned. Indeed, as he strode along the sandy beach, the ocean stretching out flat on his left, he couldn't think of anything as level as this down south. There was always an undulation to one degree or another.

Main Beach, North Stradbroke Island

Then again, this was not so different to living at Hotham. The environment was very different, true, but his attitude to it was not. He was facing it on his own terms. He was respecting it, learning about it, making it work for him - mastering it, even. But no. He could never say that. The natural environment, with all its wildness, unpredictability and, yes, occasional danger, could never be mastered. It was a mistake to think it could.

Bill was making his way in a new world, soaking it all up, gratefully receiving all it had to offer, learning, learning, learning, all the time. It was a new, exciting challenge.

13
A Leathery Meal

Something a little unusual caught Bill's eye as he wandered along the beach near North Gorge. He bent down to have a closer look. It was a large, rounded shell containing a fleshy animal. He thought he had heard of these before - the melo, or sea snail. Bill was excited to have another opportunity to experiment with consumption of the local fauna and flora. It helped to satisfy his boundless curiosity - and also saved him money!

He took the melo home and removed the animal from its shell. He cut off the fleshy foot and placed it in a pot of boiling water. He made a note, too, to put the shell safely to one side, and clean it later. The size of a small bucket, it was sure to come in handy in some way. No wonder these creatures were known as bailers!

Bill gave the melo plenty of time to be well and truly cooked. It was a big animal, and he didn't want to discover it was still raw in the middle. Eventually, he decided it had had long enough. He fished it out with a long pair of tongs and placed it on his plate. He proceeded to cut it into pieces and eat it. The taste was reasonable, but it was extremely tough and leathery. Each piece required a lot of chewing!

It had been an interesting experiment, but he couldn't see himself repeating it in a hurry.

Receipt from Bill's solicitor, Joseph Daily, for balance of money due for purchase of hut

JOSEPH E. DAILY, LL.B.
BARRISTER & SOLICITOR

TELEPHONE: MYRTLEFORD 125
VISITS BRIGHT, TUESDAYS, 1.30 P.M.–4 P.M.

No. 7054

CLYDE STREET
MYRTLEFORD

17 – 2 – 1955

Re H Maddison from Spargo

Received by CASH/CHEQUE *from* H. Maddison

the sum of One hundred and fifty-eight *pounds*

seven *shillings* —— *pence*

being balance of purchase money £150-0-0 due to Mr. Spargo and £8-5-0 costs plus 2/- exchange

£ 158 : 7 : –

VICTORIA 3d STAMP DUTY

JOSEPH E. DAILY

per V Hocking

Trust A/c.

Special Receipt Form. Authorised by The Law Institute of Victoria.

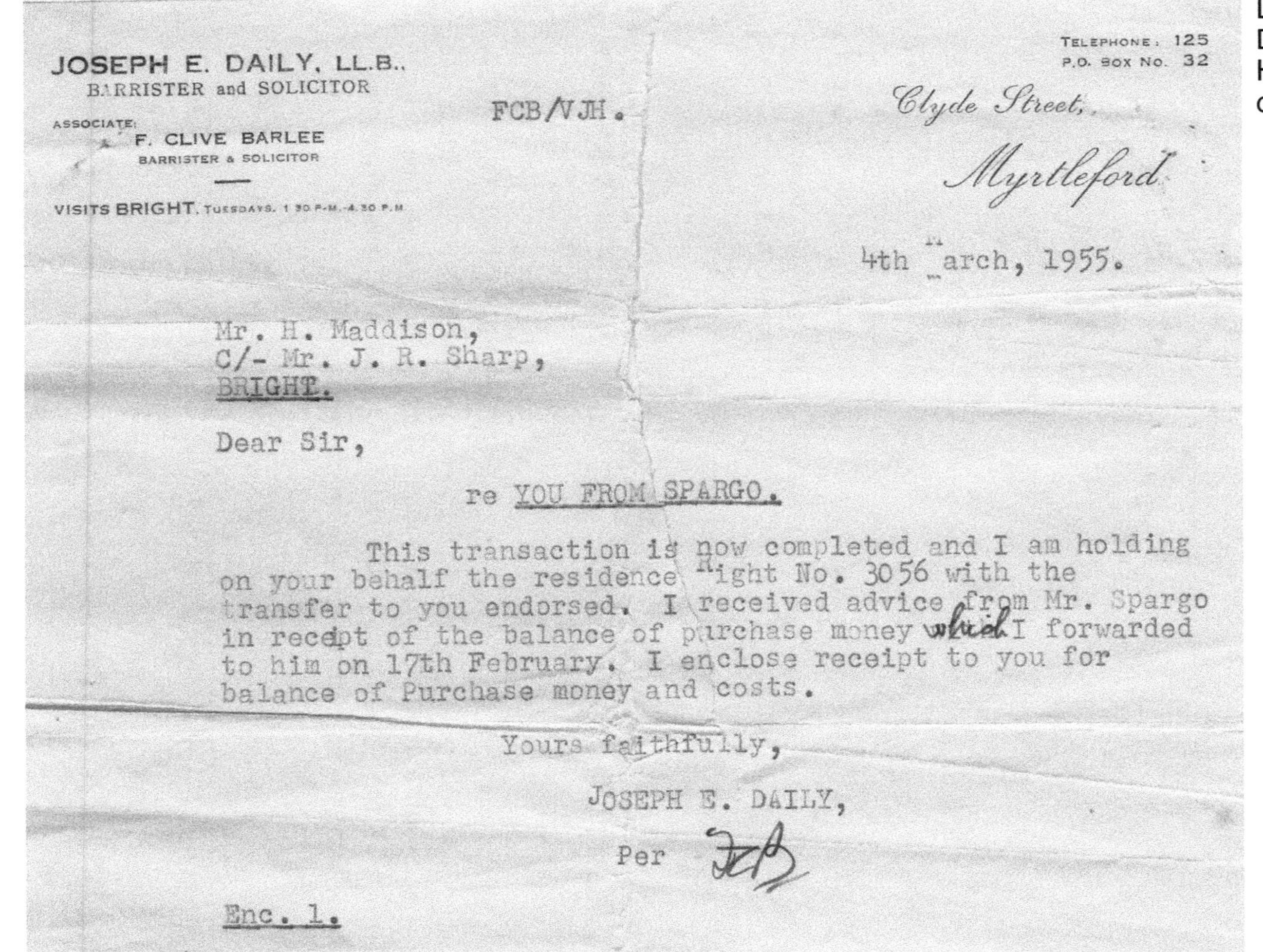

JOSEPH E. DAILY, LL.B.,
BARRISTER and SOLICITOR

ASSOCIATE:
F. CLIVE BARLEE
BARRISTER & SOLICITOR

VISITS BRIGHT, TUESDAYS, 1.30 P.M.–4.30 P.M.

TELEPHONE: 125
P.O. BOX NO. 32

FCB/VJH.

Clyde Street,
Myrtleford.

4th March, 1955.

Mr. H. Maddison,
C/- Mr. J. R. Sharp,
BRIGHT.

Dear Sir,

re YOU FROM SPARGO.

This transaction is now completed and I am holding on your behalf the residence Right No. 3056 with the transfer to you endorsed. I received advice from Mr. Spargo in receipt of the balance of purchase money which I forwarded to him on 17th February. I enclose receipt to you for balance of Purchase money and costs.

Yours faithfully,

JOSEPH E. DAILY,

Per FCB

Enc. 1.

Letter from Joseph Daily confirming Harold's purchase of the hut from Bill

14
Letter to Harold 14th March 1955

Harold had been feeling quite despondent about his correspondence with Bill when his next letter arrived. He had replied to Bill's last letter about a month after receiving it, now here was Bill's reply nearly five months later! Still, better late than never. Furthermore, he was reassuring Harold that he did not find his correspondence boring - quite the opposite, in fact. It was comforting to read how closely Bill related to Harold's quest for gold around Golden Point. He even sounded a bit more positive about the hydraulic sluicing, suggesting the hose that Harold had purchased could make the difference. He was impressed that Harold had been able to buy it second-hand, as new hoses were so expensive.

A peavey

Harold's fire hoses, presumably (photos taken in 1987)

Bill explained how he had been able to map the course of the ancient gold-bearing stream in the area quite precisely and repeated his instructions about sluicing the soil and gravel off when there was plenty of water, then scraping the rock crevasses in the drier months. Again he referred to the difficulty of removing snow gum stumps, and the need for heavy tools - a peavey or cant hook to lift them, as well as an axe and mattock. He included in the letter...*an outline sketch of the various directions in which the old streams flowed - on the course of which you will get more or less gold.*

Again, he expressed his support for Harold's plans for the cabin. He made the point that the lower part of the fireplace, being basalt, would store heat well. This would help the hot water service function effectively.

He told Harold that the wet season in Queensland had been unusually dry, and that water was short at Point Lookout. People were busy carting domestic water, and the level of Bill's well was now ten feet below the surface. He explained that the garden took most of his water, and he now had watermelons weighing as much as 30 pounds. He expressed disappointment with the letting of his two cottages but added that he wasn't planning to advertise them until he had the septic tank installed.

He thanked Harold for his offer to use the cabin at any time. He said his health was good and, if it remained so, he should be able to visit sometime. The fishing had been quiet, so he was planting seeds - beans, peas and more tomatoes.

He reminded Harold that, in addition to the shire rates, he had to pay the Lands Department five shillings on 15th December every year and that, like a mining lease, no notice was ever given. He apologised for the scrappiness of his letter and wished Harold and his wife the best of luck in their pursuit of gold.

Fireplace, Spargo's Hut (photo taken in 1982)

He added two P.S.s. The first suggested that Mrs Maddison would enjoy being out near the cabin...*especially when you can get on to a place where you can show her some slugs lying on the surface after a washing off - there is always a thrill about it.*

The second reminded Harold to stock the cabin with plenty of food in the autumn, in case he was snowed in during the winter - a sobering thought!

Bill's map, showing the course of the ancient gold-bearing stream near the hut

15
Pandanus

Bill contemplated the large pandanus fruit he held in his hands. He had heard that they were edible. The pandanus tree - the screw pine - fascinated him. The thick, woody roots left the central stem way above the ground and buttressed it against the howling winds that swept along the coast, and the shifting sands below. Perhaps more than any other type of vegetation, the pandanus symbolised the difference between his new life at Stradbroke Island, and his old life at Mt Hotham. There, the dominant tree was the snow gum. There were certainly no snow gums here! He tugged at a segment of the fruit, gently pushing it back and forth, until it came free in his hand. The inner part was soft and yellow. He placed it in his mouth and sucked - oily, and slightly sweet. Not bad!

A pandanus tree near North Gorge, Point Lookout

16
A Maritime Rescue

Bill squinted out over the water, shielding his eyes from the sun. His fishing rod lay on the sand beside him. A flash of unexpected movement had caught his attention. What was it? Yes, out there. He saw it again. It looked like a ship, and on it, several moving figures!

This was familiar territory. How many times had he rescued people caught out in blizzards at Mt Hotham? He had lost count. Bill Spargo - the alpine bushman who regularly rescued others but never required rescue himself. Old instincts kicked into life. The geography was different, of course, but the emotional terrain was the same.

It always felt good to rescue people, but it was more than that. It also elevated his standing in the community. Bill had been respected at Hotham for his ability to navigate and survive in blizzards better than anyone. He knew the folds of the hills so well, he could tell where he was even when he couldn't see them. It wasn't just experience. It was natural ability. Stradbroke, of course, did not present the same opportunities. At least it hadn't - until now. Once he had made up his mind, Bill wasted no time.

He ran back up the steep dune behind the beach as fast as he could. The path was narrow and rough, and soon he was sweating. Once he reached the sandy two-wheeled track that served as the road through town, he began running from door to door, rousing the fishermen. He knew where they all lived. His message was the same at every door.

"Emergency! Emergency! Shipwreck!"

Slowly the fishermen gathered. They agreed on a boat to take out - a strong boat that could brave the surf. Questions crossed their anxious minds. How many people were there? Where had they come from? Why had they not been spotted before now?

Still, Bill Spargo was not a man to trifle with. He knew the island well and was never panicked. He had to be taken seriously.

*

Alas for Bill, the 'figures on the wrecked ship' were not human beings. They were seals, and the ship was an old wreck.

[PHO]NE 6

BRIGHT HOLIDAY FLATS

(J. R. SHARP, PROP.)

Self Contained Furnished Flats

Hot and Cold Water
Electric Stoves, Toasters, Etc.
Own Internal Sewered Toilet Block
Inner Spring Mattresses· Wood Fires
Laundry with Electric Washing Machines

GAVAN STREET,
BRIGHT, Vic.

Jan 10th 1956

C. V. Hunter Esq.
Inspector
Lands Dept.
Omeo.

Dear Sir

Enclosed please find P.N. 5/- renewal fee on Residence Area Right No 3056. due 16th ultimo.

I asked my solicitor, Mr Haley of Myrtleford, to find out for me, to whom I had to forward the fee to. Thank you for your letter.

Must I pay yearly or can I pay the fee for say five or ten years ahead?

Thanking you
Yrs Faithfully.
Harold A. Maddison

Mr Maddison.
Rental is yearly in advance.
C V Hunter

- When booking Flats please state number of persons.
- Cutlery and Linen not Supplied. Meals Available in the Town.
- Groceries and Bread will be in your Flat on arrival. Advise Requirements.

Letter from Harold to the Lands Department containing annual payment, and asking for advice about future payments

Receipt from Lands Department for Harold's annual payment

District E omeo

DEPARTMENT OF CROWN LANDS AND SURVEY

Jan 16th 1956 Nº 22907

Received by Cash / Cheque from — H A Meddison the sum of — pounds Five shillings — pence, being payment on account of amounts due in respect of

Allotment ...... Section ...... Parish Hotham

£ : 5/- : Renewal to 16.12.56

£ : : (RA 3056)

£ : :

£ : :

£ : 5/-

ORIGINAL
To be handed to Person paying

A V Hunter for Accountant

This Receipt must be produced when making next payment.

W. M. Houston, Government Printer, Melbourne.

16th Feb., 1956.
Right No. 3056.

Department of Crown Lands & Survey.

Sir,

In reply to your letter of the 20th December addressed to my Head Office I desire to inform you that Mr. H. A. Maddison of Bright has a Right to occupy an area of land in the Omeo district and the renewal fee has been paid to renew occupancy to 16/12/1956.

It is expected that the yearly renewal fee of five shillings will be paid on due date without an account being forwarded.

Yours faithfully,

(Sgd.) Land Officer.

J. E. Daily, Esq.,
Barrister & Solicitor,
Clyde St., Myrtleford.

Letter from Lands Department to Joseph Daily confirming Harold's "Right to occupy an area of land in the Omeo district..."

17
Letter to Harold 9th March 1956

Harold received his latest letter from Bill with feelings of relief. Bill hadn't replied to his letter of 21st February but had replied straight away to his letter of 3rd March. Their correspondence was back on track. Bill was pleased to hear that Harold had found his sketch of the ancient streams useful. He reiterated the pleasure that Harold's letters gave him, taking him back to his own days poking around the hut, looking for gold, some twenty years earlier. He reminded Harold of the large numbers of copperhead snakes in the vicinity and advised him to always carry a snake bite kit. He also mentioned a large dead tree that had prevented him from working in one promising area for fear it would fall on him. He suggested that the spring would provide Harold with plenty of water for sluicing throughout November and December. He congratulated Harold on the excellent map that he had sent him, on which Bill had added his own suggestions and comments, and was returning. He offered more detailed advice on where Harold might - and might not - find gold. He finished saying he looked forward to hearing more of Harold's progress.

Highland copperhead snake

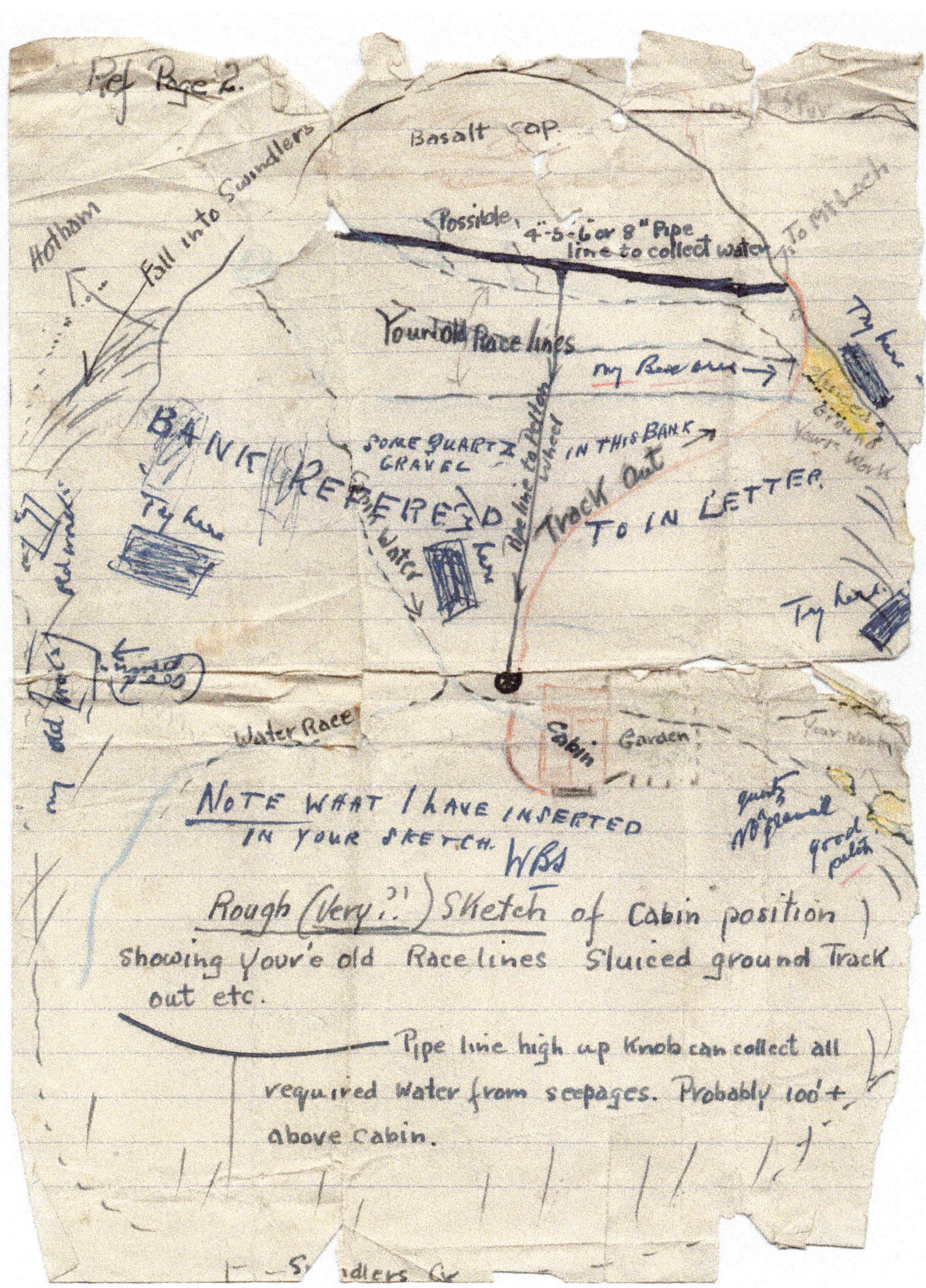

Harold's map, with Bill's additions

18
The Search for Cowries

Dr Robert Paterson gazed out to the rocks at the end of the point, and saw a familiar figure, stooped over, and looking down at the ground. Paterson had trained as a radiologist and had bought a house at the small holiday resort of Point Lookout to serve as an escape from the daily grind of reading x-rays and picking them up off the floor after they had escaped from the clasps that held them to the viewing screen. He had been coming there since 1948, when the permanent population had only been about twenty.

Paterson knew the figure on the rocks to be Bill Spargo. He had been aware of him for several years now and had discussed him with some of the locals. He was not really a part of the community, but he caused no trouble, and people admired the way he walked such vast distances along the coastline, keeping to himself all the time. No doubt today he was once again searching for cowrie shells, as he so often was seen to be doing.

19
Jasper and Agate

Bill sat at his table, a small collection of stones in front of him. He picked up each in turn, rolling it over in his hands. Yes, he had picked up a nice collection of jasper and agate stones during his long walks along the rocks. Some were better than others, naturally, but he could see that quite a few of them had good potential. With careful cutting and patient polishing, many could be turned into beautiful pieces.

Was this another path he should go down? There was no doubt that activity was his best friend. It was idleness that brought on that empty, hollow feeling that he strove so hard to dispel. Yet surely, he was already active enough? The garden, with its beautiful crop of vegetables, already kept him very busy. Besides, he would need to purchase a saw and grinder, neither of which were likely to be cheap. The work was not without its risks, either - flying bits of rock, and silica dust to avoid.

No, he had enough on his plate already. It was more than enough to keep the blues away...most of the time.

20
Letter to Harold 6th June 1956

Again, Bill had replied fairly promptly to Harold's letter of 14th May.

(I)...*found it full of interest to me from start to finish - I wish I was as good and as patient as you are at letter writing - most of my letter writing is in spasms, I would be a poor hand at been a regular correspondent.*

He told Harold how busy he was, and how interesting he found the life at Stradbroke Island. His main activities were his garden, fishing, and prospecting.

I was about to take up even yet another interest lately - that of lapidary work - the cutting and polishing of semi precious and precious stones - however I've had to pull myself up with a jerk as I have suddenly realised that one can just over do anything and make life too much of a business all the time. There is an appreciable amount of...jasper and agate here and I have already accumulated a good stock of nice pieces in the rough...

He expressed interest in the progress Harold was making with the road to the cabin *and some pieces of the furniture - yes that gramophone cabinet was a nice piece of work - it was made by my late brother Cecil just about 30 years ago from some choice South Gippsland Blackwood that I procured while supervising road construction work there - I gave the timber and paid the brother £25- for it when a £ was a £. Re your suggestion it should make a beautiful Radiogram - all the wood is solid - did you get the beautiful legs that belong to it - they were left up overhead in the cabin. I had forgotten for the time being about those paper documents and photographs etc that I had left there. I had not thought of disposing of the place when I left there last. I would be obliged Harold if you would kindly hold them for me for the present and if I'm unable to get down next summer I will get you to forward them up to me.*

He acknowledged Harold's frustration that he could not get access to much of the surrounding area because it was subjected to mining leases that were not being worked.

When I struck gold on that Red Robin area I could have pegged the whole country-side and started a boom on the strength of the "RR" (Red Robin) and (in) fact I was asked to do it but refrained knowing full well that I could not handle properly more than the "RR" - "OA" (One Alone). I would have been better off if I had only stuck to the one early in the piece. The domestic upheaval I had after the war agravated my position regarding the mines and I was glad to get away from it all - I should have kept all the property in my own name, however that's all over and done now.

Harold had let Bill know that Evelyn was trying to sell her half share of the One Alone, and Bill suggested that Harold make him an offer for his half share.

I will be very glad to get something out of the remains of the wreck and can well do with a little more cash to finish things off properly here. If my wife has any sense at all, she should take a small offer for her interest too.

He gave Harold the address of J P L Kenny, the former Victorian Chief Government Geologist, through whom Evelyn communicated

He expressed once again his desire to visit Harold and show him everything he knew about the gold and the best location for the road, though he made the point that the trip would have to pay for itself. He suggested he might be able to work for Norm Staff at the Red Robin mine during the summer. (Norm and his wife Lillian had bought the Red Robin from Bill and Evelyn in 1952.) He suggested that if Norm got his bulldozer out the following summer it would be a great opportunity to complete the road to the cabin.

Bill said he would enjoy visiting all his *old haunts*. He made it clear he would not be expecting any financial reward for his advice. He would not be expecting a share in any of the gold Harold might discover as the result of Bill's assistance. Seeing Harold - or any other prospector - having success would be reward enough. *It would be quite pointless for me to hold back on anything I know.*

He confessed that he got no more than 100 ounces of gold from the area around the cabin. Most lots were about five ounces. The best was fourteen. He again made the point that Harold might *stumble on* (the) *odd small patch or two by getting over a lot of ground with the pipes and hose* but *I would repeat again that I don't think there is anything truly payable left in the area.*

> The gold price in Australia in 1938 (around the time Bill probably stopped looking for gold around the cabin) was £8 per ounce (earlier years were similar, or a bit less), so 100 ounces would have made about £800. A pound in 1938 was worth the equivalent of about $112 in 2025. This means he made about $90,000 in total. This might sound like a lot, but he built the cabin in 1933, so spent about six years looking for gold there. (He may well have been looking for gold in that area before he built the cabin, but let's leave it at six years.) That averages out as about $15,000 per year - not really a lot of money.

Bill referred again to the road into the cabin, saying the original track had been much higher, but that more recently he had used a lower track, over on the cabin side. He referred to some tall snow gums near the head of his water race that needed to be removed. It would be much easier with the bulldozer.

Traces of the partially completed road were visible in 2006.

Ideally, Bill would like to be there with Harold to establish the line of the road himself, as he had been over it in his mind so many times.

Bill once again shared Harold's frustration with people who held leases but did not work them. He suggested that *perhaps they could be shaken up through a strongly worded article in the local press.* He felt confident about the future of the Red Robin, though. *I'm pretty sure that the Staffs will shake things up at the Red Robin next summer.* He once again made the point that, even though he no longer had any financial interest in the area around Mt Hotham, he was as keen as anyone to see its gold-bearing potential fulfilled. He referred once again to the One Alone, suggesting that Harold buy both him and Evelyn out. He appreciated the fact that neither Harold - nor anyone else - had criticised Bill for not working on the One Alone himself in recent years. He suggested to Harold that he talk to Clarrie Keating about the One Alone, as Keating had worked on it. He also said that he was sorry to hear Clarrie had not been well lately. (Clarrie had worked for Bill at the Red Robin.) He asked Harold to keep in touch and offered to help as much as he could. He was pleased to hear Harold had already had some success with his hydraulic sluicing method. He asked Harold to let him know if he had failed to answer any of the questions in Harold's *long letter.*

He talked again about his garden.

This time of the year here is like spring in the south - everything in the garden is growing like mad - I have never seen swede turnips grow so quick or so big in my life - the lettuces are wonderful too. I note too that you are making a show on your garden down there.

He added a P.S.

I nearly overlooked your enquiry about the rent of one of the cottages - they are £5 per week each - the tenant to bring own sheets and cutlery. Let me know promptly at about what time it would be wanted and whether this winter or next.

These extra rooms were most likely built by Maddison. They have since fallen down or been removed.

21
The Cry of the Curlew

Bill lay awake and listened to the cry of the bush stone-curlew. The night was still, with only the curlew to break the silence. Bill often found himself waking in the middle of the night. Eventually, he would fall asleep once again. Meanwhile, he listened to the curlew.

Its cry was piercing. No wonder the early settlers often mistook it for the anguished cry of a woman or child. His thoughts turned to Evelyn. Was this the echo of her spirit, traversing the hemispheres? Perhaps it was. Perhaps it was. How had things gone so wrong between them? Had he expected too much of her? It didn't matter now. She was there, and he was here, and that was all there was to it.

But where was he? A long, long way from the mountains he knew and loved, that was for sure. There was much to like about his new environment - the wildness of the coast, the rich array of fauna and flora, the warm climate, the spectacular growth of his vegetables. He had never been able to grow vegetables like this in Victoria. Indeed, he had barely been able to grow vegetables at all!

But this was not home. This was not where his heart lay, and it never would be. Moreover, he was trapped here. His dwindling funds would not allow him to take a holiday down there, and the prospect of finding work somewhere in the mountains was looking remote. He could move back to Victoria, but where would he live, and what would he do? Both his cabin and the mine were sold now. No, he was stuck here, for better or for worse. The trick was to keep busy, distract himself from the unfortunate nature of his position.

Bill opened his eyes a moment later - or so it seemed. The sun was already up. He heard the familiar sound of a kookaburra. That was more like it! He hadn't heard them much around Mt Hotham, but it took him right back to his childhood days in Bairnsdale. He had heard plenty of kookaburras then.

Bill tossed aside the bedclothes and stood up. There was work to do!

The bush stone-curlew

22
Ted Staff

Ted Staff relaxed in his chair, a cup of tea in one hand, a biscuit in the other. He was impressed. Bill Spargo looked an absolute picture of health. His skin was tanned, and he looked as shiny as a new shilling. His accommodation was unconventional, but he had made it work for him very well. They were sitting under Bill's water tank. He had walled the area in. The floor was considerably larger than the ceiling, and the walls sloped in on all four sides. The ceiling was about twelve feet high, and a large central strut of cypress pine, about fifteen inches in diameter, held the tank above them. Bill had left the bark on and covered it with several coats of varnish. It looked beautiful.

The trunk of the cypress pine

Bill had his bunk at one end, and his kitchen utensils at the other. Down one wall he had created a series of cells, in which he stored his many books. The bottom cells protruded further from the wall than the top cells so that, altogether, they formed a roughly vertical line. Ted was not surprised at the extent of Bill's library. He had always been a man who read and studied extensively.

Ted was visiting his wife's family in Brisbane for a holiday. It made sense to take the ferry across to Stradbroke Island for the day and visit old Bill. His father-in-law had joined him. They didn't have long, though - only a couple of hours. Then they would have to take the ferry back to Brisbane.

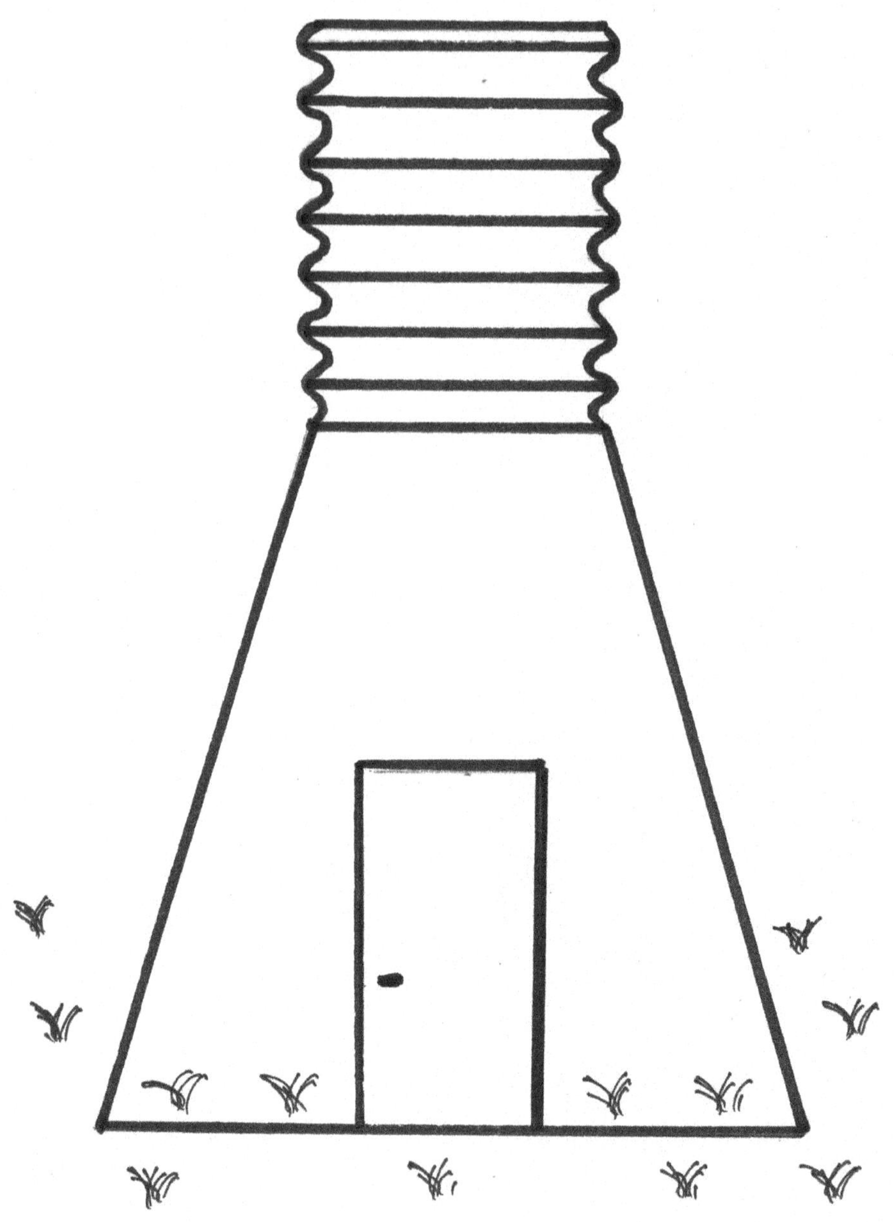

Bill lived under his water tank at Point Lookout.

Bill showed them the little cottage he had built to serve as a guest house. It had weatherboard walls, and an iron roof. He was particularly proud of its water supply. He had sunk a well and tapped into a freshwater spring. He was one of the few residents at Point Lookout - perhaps the only one - to have his own personal supply of fresh water. He piped it across to the cottage. Point Lookout was a busy holiday resort, and there didn't appear to be any difficulty attracting guests to stay there.

It was almost a decade now since Ted had last seen Bill. He had worked for him as cook at the Red Robin Mine for three months during the summer of 1949/50. He knew of Bill's domestic troubles, the breakdown of his marriage, the decision to sell the mine and move to Queensland. He was anxious to see how he was getting on. Yes indeed, Ted was most impressed. Bill was like a little king!

Ted Staff, at his home in Wodonga in 1987, demonstrating the 'hammer and tap' method used to drill for gold at the Red Robin Mine when he was working there. (Normally this is done by two men. One wields the hammer, while the other turns the drill.)

23
The Aroma of Success

Bill stood beside his vegetable garden and inhaled deeply. The rich smell of burning peat filled his nostrils. It did not appeal to everyone, he knew that well enough. He heard the complaints. It was music to his nose, though. People weren't burning peat for the hell of it. It was a good, cheap fuel for the combustion stoves that so many people owned, and if the smell was rather pungent, then so be it. That was the price you had to pay. For Bill, though, it was no price at all. No. To him, it was the smell of productivity, the aroma of personal success. It didn't generate much in the way of income, but it was certainly better than nothing. The main thing was, he had made an important contribution to the lives of the local community. That made him feel pleased, and proud.

PEAT DEPOSIT, NORTH STRADBROKE ISLAND

Queensland Government Mining Journal, March 20,1958 (Courtesy the Department of Natural Resources and Mines, Manufacturing and Regional and Rural Development (Queensland Government))

PEAT DEPOSIT, NORTH STRADBROKE ISLAND.

By H. G. S. Cribb, B.Sc., Assistant Chief Government Geologist.

This report by Mr. H. G. S. Cribb, Assistant Chief Government Geologist, places on record the occurrence of a bed of peat—the first in Queensland—at the northern end of North Stradbroke Island. The bed of peat where uncovered is 12 ft. thick and it is said to have been proved by boring to extend over an area of 100 acres. After drying the peat has a calorific value of between 8,000 and 9,000 B.T.U./lb. It makes a serviceable slow-combustion fuel and it is being exploited in a small way for this purpose.

—A.K.D.

Some four years ago, attention was drawn to an occurrence of peat on North Stradbroke Island, when local residents, Messrs. W. R. Taylor and W. B. Spargo, submitted samples for examination and proximate analysis. A study of pollen content by Miss K. M. Pike (1954) indicated its age as probably Pliocene or younger.

small swamp lying some two chains from its head at an elevation of approximately 100 ft. above sea level.

At the gully head, the deposit has been exposed over a length of 15 ft. to show a 4 ft. section of peat overlain by up to 3 ft. of unconsolidated grey-white sand, in the lowest foot of which carbonaceous matter is admixed. Some 40 ft. downstream, the bottom 5 ft. of the deposit has been opened in the bed of the gully. Although the middle section is covered by sand, there is no reason to suppose that it does not consist of peat also and the total thickness is therefore estimated to be 12 ft. Examination of the floor of the seam was hampered by water accumulation, but material recovered by shovel consisted of dark-grey sand.

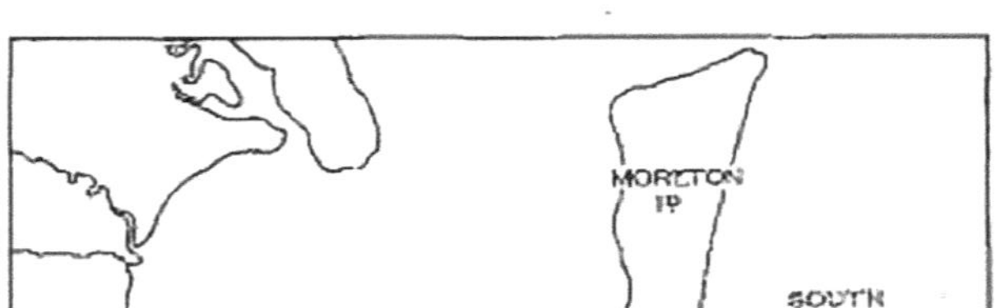

24
Letter to Harold
17th December 1957

Bill began by wishing Harold *the compliments of the season.* He told Harold he had written him a long letter on 24th September *with my comments on your plan of the location in Cicada Gully.* (This letter has been lost.) He hoped this venture had been successful, as he expected the water supply to have largely dried up by now. He looked forward to hearing further news.

He explained that they were *in the throes of a wicked drought here in Q'land, here at Pt Lookout we are facing a grim position regarding water if it doesn't rain before Xmas eve. The public water supply which is mainly for the big camping area - has given out, it will mean no water no campers which will be a blow to the business people - many of the holiday homes are also out of water, I'm lucky, having the deep well it will enable me to just get by over the holiday, with a little care.*

He had had his own lawns *up to near perfection,* but now *the grass is all brown and looks dead.* Very strong hot winds were making the situation much worse.

...all is quite depressing and most people are moaning and looking as miserable as they can, as if that will help things.

He expressed his hope that the weather was better in the Ovens Valley. He said he remained fit and well, however.

I seem to be getting further and further away from the Bright - H'ville district and hear very few items of news from down there these days. I would be pleased to hear any of the recent happenings down there when you are writing, its only the Southern news that's of any interest to me.

He wondered how they were getting on at the Red Robin. He said he had no further news to tell, so he would *cut this letter short.* He finished by wishing Harold and Mrs Maddison *the best of luck for Xmas and the New Year.*

25
Hard up

Bill stood at the bow of the trawler and felt the wind race across his bald head. He had reluctantly taken his hat off before it blew off but could feel the sun burning his scalp in spite of the cooling effect of the wind. They'd been good to him, these fishermen, taking him across Moreton Bay from Amity on the island to Wynnum Creek on the mainland pretty much whenever he'd needed them to. He had come to predict their movements well. It was no skin off their nose. He'd begun by offering them fresh home-grown vegetables in return but felt they'd taken them more out of kindness than any real need. In recent times, he hadn't even bothered with that. It certainly saved him the cost of a ferry ride from Amity. He enjoyed the rhythmic sway of the boat and the steady chug of the engine.

Yes, money was tight these days. He'd come a long way from the glory days of the Red Robin, when the world seemed to be at his feet, the opportunities limitless. How widely his imagination had stretched back then! He had had dreams of other reefs, an endless chain of buried gold stretching across a great swathe of Gippsland. Alas, they had all come to naught. There was only the Red Robin, and even that fell away sharply in richness the deeper they dug. It had been so rich at the surface, perhaps he had got a bit carried away...

He was selling fresh water from his spring to the campers these days. He didn't feel particularly good about it, but every little bit helped. He had been quite generous in the past, giving away many of his vegetables - tomatoes, lettuces, turnips, pumpkins. Those days were gone now. Fortunately, many of his nutritional needs could be found in the natural world close to his home. It wasn't the most exciting of diets, but it certainly helped to keep the wolf from the door.

He could see the mouth of the creek slowly opening before them. He much preferred the company of the rough and ready fishermen to the giggling, gawping tourists on the ferry, anyway. He was starting to feel excited now. It would be good to catch up once again with Elsie and her family.

26
One Last Look Around...

Bill walked gingerly along the headland and down towards Whale Rock. The spring in his step, which had served him so well for so long, had vanished...and it had happened so quickly. He had felt unwell for a couple of months now. It had begun so subtly that he wondered if he had imagined it, but it had soon become undeniable. A cramping pain in his abdomen. His appetite had fallen away, and then he had begun to lose weight. He was aware that he had very little fat on him at the best of times. He didn't have a lot to lose. He could feel his strength ebbing, and with it, his very zest for life.

Picking his way carefully down the rocks, he moved as close as he could to the Blowhole. He wanted to hear it again, as it sent water and wind high into the air. He watched and listened for a long time. He was filled with a sense of foreboding that could not be denied. Would this prove to be the last time he stood here and took in this magnificent view? He knew what awaited him, and it terrified him - the city, doctors, white coats, stainless steel. People being kind because they were paid to do so.

His thoughts turned back to the hut he had built with Cecil all those years ago...the years spent with Evelyn...the fight against the fire...the thrill of the discovery of the Red Robin gold reef. He had never imagined, the last time he had left it, that he would never return. Events had overtaken him so quickly. He thought, too, of all that he had left behind. To be honest, there was not much in there that he really needed - he had already demonstrated that by adapting so well to his new life at Point Lookout - but there was plenty that was of sentimental value. It would have been nice to have had some mementoes of the south during these last few years. It hardly mattered now. He was happy for Harold to keep the bed, likewise the table and chairs. The coolgardie safe would have been handy, though. Keeping food cool up here had been an even bigger challenge than at Hotham. Still, he'd managed to knock up another without too much difficulty. Perhaps more than anything, he missed the gramophone cabinet that Cecil had made from that beautiful piece of blackwood. He definitely could have made good use of that up here. It would have been nice to have been able to play a bit of music in the evenings, and it certainly would have added a decorative touch to his home. He hoped that Harold loved it as much as he did and had looked after it well.

Oh, how he wished the view before him was Mt Hotham...the view across Swindlers Valley to Mt Loch. That was where his heart lay. He ached to see it once again, but he knew he never would. So many times he had laid plans to return during the summer months, but they had all come to naught. He simply hadn't been able to raise the funds. He cursed himself now for his prudence. If he had known this was going to come upon him so suddenly, he would have thrown caution to the wind and simply got on a plane. Too late, he was learning the lesson. Strike while you can. Who knows what lies around the corner?

Well, it was too late for such regrets now. This was not his home. Yes, he had lived here for the past five years, but it was not his home. Not really. Still, it was beautiful. That could not be denied. It was unfair to compare the coast to the mountains. They both contained their inner dignity and serenity. It might not be Mt Hotham, but it was still nature in the raw, and that is what Bill loved the most, what he had dedicated his life to, in a way.

A long, involuntary sigh issued from his lips. He turned and slowly picked his way back up the rocks and through the pandanus trees to home. He needed to pack his bag and didn't want to miss his lift to town. A kangaroo with joey watched him silently as he passed.

27
A Disappointing Sick Bed Conversation

Norm Staff sat at the airport terminal waiting for the plane to take him back to Melbourne from Brisbane. He gazed out at the grey sky. It matched his mood. He had felt quite buoyant on the flight up, but his dreams and hopes had now turned to ashes. Norm was convinced that Bill had discovered a gold reef every bit as rich as the Red Robin near his hut at Golden Point. Why else had he spent so much time back at Golden Point while working at the mine? He slept in his hut there every night. It was a good two hour walk each way. Probably more. It made no sense, unless... The mine workers had discussed it amongst themselves many times.

True, Bill did not owe Norm any favours. Then again, they went back a long way, and their stories were intertwined. Norm had worked at the Red Robin himself. So had his younger brother, Ted. Then Norm and his wife, Lil, had purchased the Red Robin from Bill and Evelyn back in 1952. To be honest, it was not something Norm had really wanted to do, but Lil had the money, and she was keen to help Evelyn out of a tight spot. Evelyn needed money badly, and nobody else was showing any interest in buying the Red Robin Mine. Norm was sure Bill would want to see the reef worked, and now, lying in a hospital bed, and dying of cancer, he was never going to be able to work it himself.

But no. Norm had come away empty-handed. He wasn't prepared to raise the subject himself, but he had dropped a number of hints. Bill had not responded to any of them. He clearly wasn't prepared to tell Norm anything. Had he done something to offend Bill over the years? He couldn't think of anything, but Bill was notoriously sensitive, and it was quite possible. The secret may now die with Bill. It was frustrating, and very disappointing.

Norm Staff at the Red Robin Mine, around 1950

28
Evelyn

Bill lay back on his pillow, eyes closed. His nostrils were filled with the powerful smell of disinfectant that pervaded his world these days. His surroundings were familiar enough to him, even though he had only been here a few days. The walls were stark, and white. A small, framed picture of the Crucifixion hung on the wall behind him. This building was only a few years old, but it had clearly been built with economy in mind. His dinner sat on a wheeled trolley to the right of his bed, where he had pushed it. It wasn't a bad meal for a hospital - several slices of roast beef, some thin gravy, roast potatoes and turnips, and some boiled peas. He had had a couple of nibbles, but his appetite had deserted him completely since arriving in hospital. Indeed, it had been some time since he'd eaten a hearty meal. The weight appeared to be dripping off him. The once taut, lean muscles, of which he had been so proud, were melting away.

His thoughts, as so often was the case these days, were with Evelyn. What was she doing right now, he wondered. She was no doubt aware of his failing health - or if not, she soon would be. Norm Staff would make sure of that, if nobody else did. Lillian and Evelyn remained steadfast friends and communicated regularly across the vast distances that lay between them. He could never have imagined twenty years ago that she would play no part in his life as it drew to a close. He had loved her so much. Indeed, a decade ago, she had shared this beautiful environment with him. She had enjoyed its golden sands and warm water as much as anybody. He could hardly complain that she had not reached out to him now, though. He had certainly not reached out to her. Nor did he have any intention of doing so now. No. He had made his bed, as the saying goes.

Evelyn Spargo (nee Piper) at Stradbroke Island, 1947

There was a gnawing pain in the pit of his stomach that never let go. The morphine provided a little relief, but not for long. He tried lying on his side. It had never really helped him much, and he did not expect it to now, either, but he just felt he had to try a change in position. Should he ask for another dose? There wasn't much point. It was too soon since the last one. Besides, he had never complained about anything in the past. He wasn't about to start now.

He rolled back onto his back and gave a deep sigh. Hopefully the end would come quickly.

A Closing Word

Bill Spargo died of cancer of the stomach after a short illness at Mount Olivet Hospital, Kangaroo Point, Queensland, on 7th January 1959. He was seventy years old. The hospital had been established in 1957 for the terminally ill, especially those with limited financial resources. His old friend Warrand Begg, longstanding President of the University Ski Club, was by his side when he died.

Bill's estate amounted to £2,000 (approximately $77,000 in 2025). It was split evenly between his four nephews - Len Spargo (son of Bill's brother Cecil), Bill Wilson (son of his sister Polly) and Frank and Allan Stevens (sons of his sister Elsie). His niece Elsie (daughter of Polly) received nothing. This caused considerable family tension for some time.

Stomach cancer is rare in Australia. It is common in Japan, where diets are generally rich in fish, but poor in red meat (or at least they were back then). Was this the case for Bill also?

Like his brother, Norm, Ted Staff believed believed that Bill had found another gold reef (quoting Ted) "out Hotham way, just as good as the Red Robin." Even though Bill had not disclosed its location to Norm when he had visited him in hospital, Ted believed he had done so to some other men from Bright. "They took a bulldozer up, and they couldn't find it. They scraped the top off the ground...looking for the reef, and they couldn't find it."

Bill's letters to Harold, however, make it very clear that there was no rich gold reef in the vicinity of Mt Hotham - at least to his knowledge - other than the Red Robin.

Furthermore, Norm Staff's belief that Bill was living at the hut at Golden Point while working at the Red Robin Mine should perhaps be taken with a grain of salt. (Ted also believed this.) Bill makes no reference to this in his journal, and Evelyn, writing to Bill on 29th August 1951, refers to nobody having lived in the hut for the last ten years.

Harold Maddison died in 1972, aged 71. Power, hot water and lighting were not installed at the cabin at Golden Point. The road was not completed, and there is no evidence of a Pelton wheel in the vicinity. The cabin did not prove a success as a holiday home for Harold's family. It is not clear how much gold he found there.

Nancye Sullivan told me that her father took the blackwood gramophone cabinet to the Buffalo View Hotel in Porepunkah, where it was held in private quarters. She was not aware of its current whereabouts.

Nancye died in 1994, aged 50.

No ski jumps, at least to my knowledge, have ever been built in the vicinity of Spargo's Hut.

A sunset view of Golden Point from Hotham

Photo/Image credits

(Those not credited are by me)

Bill Spargo (courtesy Dianne Carroll - High Country Heritage/ Pioneer Portraits) - Page 2

Evelyn Piper (courtesy Kate Piper) - Page 3

Bill Spargo at the Red Robin Mine, around 1950 (courtesy Ted Staff) - Page 9

Buffalo View Hotel, Porepunkah (courtesy of the National Trust of Australia (Victoria)) - Page 12

Pelton wheel (courtesy Wikipedia) - Page 22

First page of Bill's letter to Harold... (courtesy Nancye Sullivan) - Page 25

Cnidoglanis macrocephalus... (courtesy Wikipedia/Sylke Rorhlach) - Page 30

Receipt from Bill's solicitor, Joseph Daily... (courtesy Nancye Sullivan) - Page 36

Letter from Joseph Daily... (courtesy Nancye Sullivan) - Page 37

A peavey (courtesy Wikipedia) - Page 38

Bill's map... (courtesy Nancye Sullivan) - Page 43

Letter from Harold to the Lands Department... (courtesy Nancye Sullivan) - Page 47

Receipt from Lands Department... (courtesy Nancye Sullivan) - Page 48

Letter from Lands Department to Joseph Daily... (courtesy Nancye Sullivan) - Page 49

Highland copperhead snake (courtesy Wikipedia/Will Brown) - Page 50

Harold's map, with Bill's additions (courtesy Nancye Sullivan) - Page 51

These extra rooms... (both photos courtesy Harrietville Historical Society) - Page 58

PEAT DEPOSIT, NORTH STRADBROKE ISLAND (Courtesy the Department of Natural Resources and Mines, Manufacturing and Regional and Rural Development (Queensland Government)) - Page 66

Norm Staff at the Red Robin Mine, around 1950 (courtesy Ted Staff) - Page 74

Evelyn Spargo (nee Piper) at Stradbroke Island, 1947 (photo by W. B. Spargo, courtesy Kate Piper) - Page 76

Acknowledgements

Thank you to Maggie Somerville for editing the manuscript, and for her unfailing support and enthusiasm. Valuable editorial assistance was also provided by Dr Peter Fullagar and my son, Thomas Whiteside. Thank you to Neville Spargo (Bill's great nephew, grandson of his brother, Cecil) for giving me permission to quote from Bill's letters to Harold Maddison. Thank you to long term Stradbroke Island resident Gwennie Specht for providing me with information about the island, and Bill's time there. Thank you to Robyn Downie, President of the Harrietville Historical Society, for sending me, and allowing me to publish, the photos showing the extra rooms on the hut. Thank you to Margaret Mueller (Bill Callander's daughter) and Janet Wraith for providing me with information about the Callanders' store in Wangaratta. Thank you to Fiona Stanley for another excellent book cover. Thank you to Clive Willman, Ken Harris and Dr Fullagar for providing technical advice about mining. Thank you also to Dr Fullagar for finding documentary evidence of Bill's discovery of peat on North Stradbroke Island. Thank you to Jon Hutchins (Chair, National Alpine Museum of Australia) for also providing valuable advice. Thank you to Ian Stapleton for his continued encouragement. Thank you to all at Busybird Publishing for helping me to put this book together. Finally, thank you once again to Thomas and my daughter, Lenore, for their ongoing encouragement and support.

About the Author

Stephen Whiteside has been walking and skiing through the Australian mountains for most of his life. He has also been writing for many years - mostly rhyming verse, but also short stories, and articles about Australia's history and natural environment. Many of his poems have been published in magazines or anthologies, both in Australia and overseas, or won awards. In 2014, Walker Books published a collection of his poetry for children, "The Billy that Died with its Boots On and other Australian Verse." In 2015, the book won a Golden Gumleaf for "Book of the Year" at the Australian Bush Laureate Awards during the Tamworth Country Music Festival. In 2016 he judged the Secondary School section of the Dorothea Mackellar Poetry Awards. Whiteside works as a GP in Melbourne.

Previous books by Stephen Whiteside

Pearl Bradshaw - Princess of Hotham (self-published via Busybird Publishing, 2025)

Snow, Fire and Gold - the story of Bill Spargo and Evelyn Piper's life in the Australian mountains (self-published via Busybird Publishing, 2024)

The Billy That Died With its Boots On and Other Australian Verse (Walker Books, 2014)

The "Ant Explorer" Parodies (self-published, 2010)

"The Brigadier's Horse" and other poems from the Western Front by Arthur Dean, compiled by Stephen Whiteside (self-published 2010)

The Paterson Parodies (self-published 2009)

Poems of 2008 (self-published 2009)

Early Poems and Songs (including "Omeo") (self-published 2008)

Poems of 2007 (self-published 2008)

Stephen Whiteside interviewed Pearl Bradshaw in 1987 as part of his research for 'Snow, Fire and Gold - the story of Bill Spargo and Evelyn Piper's life in the Australian mountains.' With her husband, Jim (who had died in 1981), Pearl had managed the Hotham Heights Chalet at Mt Hotham from 1937 - 45, a total of nine consecutive winters. This period had included the 1939 bushfire, which burnt almost two million hectares of the state of Victoria and cost 71 lives, and the Second World War. Reflecting on the interview afterwards, he realised that Pearl's own life had been fascinating, and returned to interview her a second time later in the year.

This is Pearl's story.

Stephen Whiteside knew that Spargo's Hut in the Australian mountains near Mt Hotham had been abandoned for many years. However, when he first visited it in 1982, he got a shock. It looked like it was still inhabited. Could he have been mistaken? Closer inspection revealed that it was, indeed, abandoned. However, its remoteness had allowed it to remain crammed full of all the items necessary for everyday living. There was a bed and pillow, a table and chairs, a Coolgardie safe, pots and pans, crockery and cutlery, a cheese grater, a fly spray pump, an oven mitt, a golf putter, books and magazines, and much, much more.

It looked to him as though a woman had lived there as well as a man. Who were these people who had lived in this one room hut above the snow line, and why? He resolved to find out...